States of America

the thirteen united

When in the Course of human events, it becomes necessary for one people to dissolve the political bands which have connected them with another, and to assume among the powers of the earth, the separate and equal station to which the Laws of Nature and of Nature's God entitle them, a decent respect to the opinions of mankind requires that they should declare the causes which impel them to the separation.

We hold these truths to be self-evident, that all men are created equal, that they are endowed by their Creator with certain unalienable Rights, that among these are Life, Liberty and the pursuit of Happiness.—That to secure these rights, Governments are instituted among Men, deriving their just powers from the consent of the governed,—That whenever any Form of Government becomes destructive of these ends, it is the Right of the People to alter or to abolish it, and to institute new Government, laying its foundation on such principles and organizing its powers in such form, as to them shall seem most likely to effect their Safety and Happiness. Prudence, indeed, will dictate that Governments long established should not be changed for light and transient causes; and accordingly all experience hath shewn, that mankind are more disposed to suffer, while evils are sufferable, than to right themselves by abolishing the forms to which they are accustomed. But when a long train of abuses and usurpations, pursuing invariably the same Object evinces a design to reduce them under absolute Despotism, it is their right, it is their duty, to throw off such Government, and to provide new Guards for their future security.—Such has been the patient sufferance of these Colonies; and such is now the necessity which constrains them to alter their former Systems of Government. The history of the present King of Great Britain is a history of repeated injuries and usurpations, all having in direct object the establishment of an absolute Tyranny over these States. To prove this, let Facts be submitted to a candid world.

He has refused his Assent to Laws, the most wholesome and necessary for the public good.— He has forbidden his Governors to pass Laws of immediate and pressing importance, unless suspended in their operation till his Assent should be obtained; and when so suspended, he has utterly neglected to attend to them.— He has refused to pass other Laws for the accommodation of large districts of people, unless those people would relinquish the right of Representation in the Legislature, a right inestimable to them and formidable to tyrants only.— He has called together legislative bodies at places unusual, uncomfortable, and distant from the depository of their public Records, for the sole purpose of fatiguing them into compliance with his measures.— He has dissolved Representative Houses repeatedly, for opposing with manly firmness his invasions on the rights of the people.— He has refused for a long time, after such dissolutions, to cause others to be elected; whereby the Legislative powers, incapable of Annihilation, have returned to the People at large for their exercise; the State remaining in the mean time exposed to all the dangers of invasion from without, and convulsions within.— He has endeavoured to prevent the population of these States; for that purpose obstructing the Laws for Naturalization of Foreigners; refusing to pass others to encourage their migration hither, and raising the conditions of new Appropriations of Lands.— He has obstructed the Administration of Justice, by refusing his Assent to Laws for establishing Judiciary powers.— He has made Judges dependent on his Will alone, for the tenure of their offices, and the amount and payment of their salaries.— He has erected a multitude of New Offices, and sent hither swarms of Officers to harrass our people, and eat out their substance.— He has kept among us, in times of peace, Standing Armies without the Consent of our legislatures.— He has affected to render the Military independent of and superior to the Civil power.— He has combined with others to subject us to a jurisdiction foreign to our constitution, and unacknowledged by our laws; giving his Assent to their Acts of pretended Legislation:— For quartering large bodies of armed troops among us:— For protecting them, by a mock Trial, from punishment for any Murders which they should commit on the Inhabitants of these States:— For cutting off our Trade with all parts of the world:— For imposing Taxes on us without our Consent:— For depriving us in many cases, of the benefits of Trial by Jury:— For transporting us beyond Seas to be tried for pretended offences:— For abolishing the free System of English Laws in a neighbouring Province, establishing therein an Arbitrary government, and enlarging its Boundaries so as to render it at once an example and fit instrument for introducing the same absolute rule into these Colonies:— For taking away our Charters, abolishing our most valuable Laws, and

should declare the causes which impel them to the separation. ———— ... ... with certain unalienable Rights; that among these are Life, Liberty and the pursuit of Happiness — ... powers from the consent of the governed, — That whenever any Form of Government becomes ... Government, laying its foundation on such principles and organizing its powers in such ... will dictate that Governments long established should not be changed for light and transient ... evils are sufferable, than to right themselves by abolishing the forms to which they are accustomed ... evinces a design to reduce them under absolute Despotism, it is their right, it is their duty, to ... over the patient sufferance of these Colonies; and such is now the necessity which constrains them ... Britain is a history of repeated injuries and usurpations, all having in direct object the establishment ... world. ———— He has refused his Assent to Laws, the most wholesome and necessary ... and pressing importance, unless suspended in their operation till his Assent should be obtained ... pass other Laws for the accommodation of large districts of people, unless those people would relinquish ... to tyrants only. ———— He has called together legislative bodies at places unusual, uncomfortable ... compliance with his measures. ———— He has dissolved Representative Houses repeatedly, for ... a long time, after such dissolutions, to cause others to be elected; whereby the Legislative powers ... -ing in the mean time exposed to all the dangers of invasion from without, and convulsions within ... -ting the Laws for Naturalization of Foreigners; refusing to pass others to encourage their migration ... Administration of Justice, by refusing his Assent to Laws for establishing judiciary powers ———— ... and payment of their salaries ———— He has erected a multitude of New Offices, and sent ... us in times of peace Standing Armies without the Consent of our legislatures ———— He has ... -with others to subject us to a jurisdiction foreign to our constitution, and unacknowledged by ... armed troops among us — For protecting them, by a mock Trial, from punishment for any ... our Trade with all parts of the world — For imposing Taxes on us without our Consent ... -seas to be tried for pretended offences ———— For abolishing the free System of English Laws in ... as to render it at once an example and fit instrument for introducing the same absolute ... altering fundamentally the Forms of our Governments ———— For suspending our own Legislatures ... — He has abdicated Government here, by declaring us out of his Protection and waging War ag— ... ... paralleled in the most barbarous ages, and totally unworthy the Head of a civilized nation ... their country, to become the executioners of their friends and Brethren, or to fall themselves by their ... inhabitants of our frontiers, the merciless Indian Savages, whose known rule of warfare, is an undis— ... have Petitioned for Redress in the most humble terms. Our repeated Petitions have been answered ... is unfit to be the ruler of a free people. Nor have We been wanting in attentions to our Britt— ... -ble jurisdiction over us. We have reminded them of the circumstances of our emigration and ... by the ties of our common kindred to disavow these usurpations, which, would inevitably int— ... consanguinity. We must, therefore, acquiesce in the necessity, which denounces our Separation ... We, therefore, the Representatives of the united States of America, in ... -tentions, do, in the Name, and by Authority of the good People of these Colonies, solemnly publish

"I am well aware of the toil and blood and treasure that it will cost us to maintain this Declaration and support and defend these states. Yet through all the gloom, I can see the rays of ravishing light and glory."

JOHN ADAMS

in a letter to his wife, Abigail
July 3, 1776

For George Walton —DM

Published by Bushel & Peck Books, a family-run publishing house in Fresno, California, that
believes in uplifting children with the highest standards of art, music, literature, and ideas.
Find beautiful books for gifted young minds at www.bushelandpeckbooks.com.

Type set in Josefi n Sans, Papercute, IM Fell English Pro, and Providence Sans Pro.

Bushel & Peck Books is dedicated to fi ghting illiteracy all over the world.
For every book we sell, we donate one to a child in need—book for book.
To nominate a school or organization to receive free books,
please visit www.bushelandpeckbooks.com.

Collage illustrations created from visuals sourced from illustrator
Albert Pinilla, public domain archives, and Shutterstock.

ISBN: 9781638190486

First Edition

Printed in China

10 9 8 7 6 5 4 3

the SIDE-BY-SIDE DECLARATION OF INDEPENDENCE

DAVID MILES

BUSHEL
& PECK
BOOKS

FRESNO, CALIFORNIA

BUILDUP TO THE DECLARATION

Welcome to your guided tour of the Declaration of Independence! We'll get to the Declaration in a minute, but hang tight; first, it's important to understand some of the events that set the stage for such a groundbreaking event.

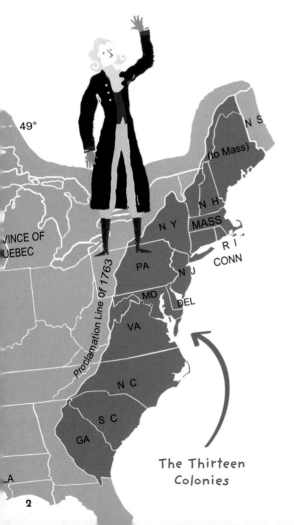

The Thirteen Colonies

COLONIES IN AMERICA

Our story begins in 1585, when Sir Walter Raleigh founded the first British colony on the island of Roanoke, now part of North Carolina. The settlers at Roanoke mysteriously disappeared (that's another tale), and a new colony was established in Jamestown, Virginia. Over the next 150 years, thirteen British colonies would appear on American soil, from New Hampshire in the north to Georgia in the south.

At first, these colonies had a great deal of freedom to govern themselves. After all, Great Britain was miles away across the Atlantic Ocean. Many colonies had governing bodies of elected representatives, like the Virginia House of Burgesses, that passed their own laws.

THE FRENCH AND INDIAN WAR

But Great Britain wasn't the only country with colonies in America. France, Spain, and other European countries wanted land and influence in America, and war eventually broke out. The French and Indian War lasted from 1754 until 1763, when the Treaty of Paris was signed. Though Great Britain won the war and most of the land east of the Mississippi River, that victory came with a cost: debt, and *lots* of it.

The British Parliament (see page 48) needed a way to pay for all the bills that were stacking up. They came up with what seemed like a brilliant idea: tax the colonies! After all, weren't the colonists the ones who benefited most from the victory?

During the French and Indian War, George Washington served as a colonel in the British army.

3

One-penny stamps had to be affixed to certain documents to make them legal. The Stamp Act was one way Parliament taxed the colonies.

TAXATION WITHOUT REPRESENTATION

That wasn't how the colonists saw it. When new taxes poured in on everything from tea to paper to glass to playing cards, they were furious. They protested the taxes and demanded representation in Parliament. Sometimes things got violent, like when American colonists tarred and feathered British tax collectors or destroyed 342 chests of tea in the Boston Tea Party (no, not *that* kind of tea party). Now it was Britain's turn to be furious. Parliament responded with laws designed to punish the colonies, like closing the Boston port and dissolving some colonial legislatures (we'll cover these punishments in more detail later).

The Boston Tea Party

THE FIRST CONTINENTAL CONGRESS

The time for action had come. In 1774, twelve of the thirteen colonies sent delegates to meet in Philadelphia and discuss what should be done. First, they decided to stop importing British goods. Then, they wrote a declaration of rights to send to Parliament.

A mural depicting the First Continental Congress meeting in Carpenters' Hall in Philadelphia, Pennsylvania.

The Second Continental Congress met in Independence Hall, also in Philadelphia.

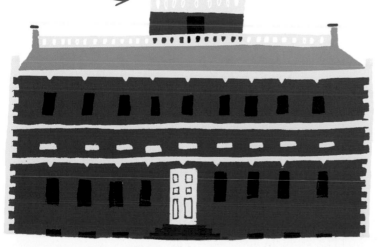

THE SECOND CONTINENTAL CONGRESS

In May of 1775, the congress met again. Parliament had ignored the declaration of rights, British troops had clashed with colonial militias at Lexington and Concord, and war was upon them. But even then, some hoped for reconciliation with Great Britain (see page 75). The colonists sent a letter to King George III (see page 27), the British king, declaring their loyalty and seeking a path to peace.

A fictional depiction of the writers of the Declaration at work. Not shown are Roger Sherman and Robert Livingston, who also helped.

Thomas Jefferson

Benjamin Franklin

John Adams

Jefferson borrowed heavily from other works. As he put it, he was "not striving for originality of principal or sentiment" but simply an "expression of the American mind." (Still, don't do this at school, kids.)

INDEPENDENCE DECLARED

But peace was not to be. Instead, King George declared that the colonists were in open rebellion and sent British troops and German mercenaries (see page 69) to fight the colonies. Support for independence among the colonists had gone from simmering to boiling, and in the summer of 1776, Congress appointed a committee to draft a declaration of independence. With Thomas Jefferson as lead writer, they laid out their frustrations with British rule and put forth their reasons for breaking ties. Congress officially declared freedom from Great Britain on July 2, 1776, and then worked for two days debating the actual wording of the Declaration. It was officially adopted by Congress on July 4, 1776, and later signed by most delegates in August.

The Declaration of Independence thrilled the colonists and united them around the war effort. Copies were sent all over the colonies to be read and celebrated.

And now, it's your turn to do just that . . .

King George's official proclamation of rebellion.

IN CONGRESS, JULY 4, 1776.
The unanimous Declaration of the thirteen united States of America.

HOW TO USE THIS BOOK

Deciphering what the Declaration of Independence is saying isn't easy, even for adults. To make it simple, this book will take you through the document one line at a time.

The red pages show the original text from the Declaration.

The blue pages provide a "plain English" translation.

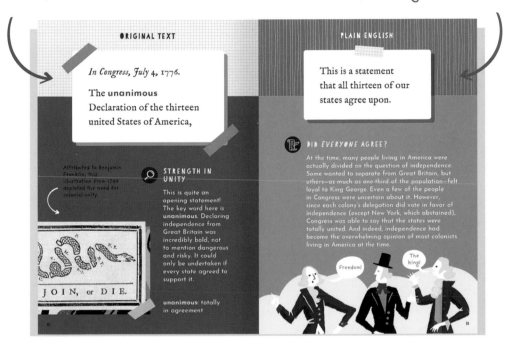

ORIGINAL TEXT

In Congress, July 4, 1776.

The **unanimous** Declaration of the thirteen united States of America,

Attributed to Benjamin Franklin, this illustration from 1764 depicted the need for colonial unity.

STRENGTH IN UNITY

This is quite an opening statement! The key word here is **unanimous**. Declaring independence from Great Britain was incredibly bold, not to mention dangerous and risky. It could only be undertaken if every state agreed to support it.

unanimous: totally in agreement

JOIN, or DIE.

PLAIN ENGLISH

This is a statement that all thirteen of our states agree upon.

DID EVERYONE AGREE?

At the time, many people living in America were actually divided on the question of independence. Some wanted to separate from Great Britain, but others—as much as one-third of the population—felt loyal to King George. Even a few of the people in Congress were uncertain about it. However, since each colony's delegation did vote in favor of independence (except New York, which abstained), Congress was able to say that the states were totally united. And indeed, independence had become the overwhelming opinion of most colonists living in America at the time.

Freedom!

The king!

You'll also find learning aids marked by these icons:

 LEARN THE HISTORY These sections will provide you with background about what was happening at the time in history.

 LOOK CLOSER These sections will challenge you to look more closely at some of the wording or concepts used in the Declaration.

 THINK DEEPER These sections will encourage you to think more critically about what the Declaration is saying and how that might apply today.

In Congress, July 4, 1776.

The **unanimous** Declaration of the thirteen united States of America,

Attributed to Benjamin Franklin, this illustration from 1754 depicted the need for colonial unity.

STRENGTH IN UNITY

This is quite an opening statement! The key word here is **unanimous**. Declaring independence from Great Britain was incredibly bold, not to mention dangerous and risky. It could only be undertaken if every state agreed to support it.

unanimous: totally in agreement

JOIN, or DIE.

This is a statement that all thirteen of our states agree upon.

 ### DID *EVERYONE* AGREE?

At the time, people living in America were divided on the question of independence. Some wanted to separate from Great Britain, but others—as much as one-third of the population—felt loyal to King George. Even a few of the people in Congress were uncertain about it. However, since each colony's delegation did vote in favor of independence (except New York, which abstained), Congress was able to claim that the states were totally united. And indeed, independence had become the overwhelming opinion of most colonists living in America at the time.

When in the Course of human events, it becomes necessary for one people to dissolve the political bands which have connected them with another, and to assume among the powers of the earth, the separate and equal station to which the Laws of Nature and of Nature's God entitle them, a decent respect to the opinions of mankind requires that they should declare the causes which **impel** them to the separation.

impel: to force someone to do something

When a group wants to separate from another group and be independent, it's polite to explain why.

Yoo-hoo! Just thought you'd like to know.

UNPRECEDENTED

When the Declaration talked about dissolving "political bands," this was a very big deal. In fact, the American Revolution marked the first time a colony won independence from its European mother country. Since then, many other countries fought for and won independence, including Mexico, Haiti, and Greece.

Jean-Jacques Dessalines, leader of the Haitian Revolution

Miguel Hidalgo y Costilla, founding father of Mexico

We hold these truths to be **self-evident**, that all men are created equal, that they are endowed by their Creator with certain **unalienable** Rights, that among these are Life, **Liberty** and the pursuit of Happiness.

self-evident: obvious; shouldn't have to be explained

unalienable: can't be taken away

liberty: freedom

Some things are just obvious: Everyone is equal, and God has given them rights. These rights include a right to live, a right to be free, and a right to be happy.

WHAT ABOUT SLAVERY?

Thomas Jefferson

It's true that many of the signers of the Declaration of Independence owned slaves. The document's main author himself, Thomas Jefferson, owned 600 slaves throughout his life. All this talk of freedom and rights might seem contradictory coming from slave owners, and in many ways, it was. This contentious topic would come up again during the Constitutional Convention, the Civil War, and on into the present day. And yet, though imperfect, we can still thank the writers for setting our nation on a course that values equality. Indeed, their very words would guide the efforts of activists hundreds of years later (see page 89).

—That to secure these rights, Governments are instituted among Men, deriving their just powers from the **consent** of the governed,

WHERE DOES POWER COME FROM?

Over thousands of years of human history, there have been many forms of government. Some governments were ruled by a monarch, like King George, who had power because of being born into a certain family. Other rulers, like the pharaohs of Egypt, claimed that their right to rule came from the gods. And other rulers kept power by having the biggest, meanest army for miles around. But what the colonists tell King George here is very significant: a government's power doesn't come from position or wealth or religion or might. It comes only from the people themselves.

A government's job is to protect these rights. Government gets its power from the approval of the people it was set up to help.

consent: agreement

THINK DEEPER

What kinds of safeguards does a government need to ensure that the power stays with the people?

—That whenever any Form of Government becomes destructive of these ends, it is the Right of the People to **alter** or to **abolish** it, and to **institute** new Government, laying its foundation on such principles and organizing its powers in such form, as to them shall seem most likely to effect their Safety and Happiness.

The Constitutional Convention was held in 1787, eleven years after the Declaration of Independence was signed.

alter: to change

abolish: to end something

institute: to establish

When a government destroys the rights of its people, the people have a right to replace it with something they think will work better.

The US Constitution

THINK DEEPER

After the Revolutionary War and an unsuccessful experience with the Articles of Confederation, America started using the government we recognize today as set up in the US Constitution. In this government, there was an elected president, an elected Congress, and a judicial system, each with powers that balanced one another. How was this different from what the colonists experienced under King George and the British Parliament? Do you think it works better? Why or why not?

Prudence, indeed, will dictate that Governments long established should not be changed for light and transient causes; and accordingly all experience hath shewn, that mankind are more disposed to suffer, while evils are sufferable, than to right themselves by abolishing the forms to which they are accustomed.

 ## A LESSON FROM HISTORY: FEUDALISM

Feudalism was very common during the Middle Ages (400s-1400s). In this system, lords—people of noble families who owned property and could hire soldiers— allowed peasants to live on their land and farm it on their behalf. In return, the lord protected the peasants with his armies. It wasn't pleasant for most, but since it was better than being killed by marauders, the system largely went unchallenged.

Of course, this shouldn't be done flippantly. After all, most people would rather deal with a bad government than try to replace it altogether.

THINK DEEPER

Read about feudalism on the opposite page. The colonists of America had it much better than the peasants of the Middle Ages, so why do you think they were so eager to upend their system for a new government? What do you think was motivating them?

Peasants work in their lord's fields.

But when a long train of abuses and **usurpations**, pursuing invariably the same Object **evinces** a design to reduce them under absolute **Despotism**, it is their right, it is their duty, to throw off such Government, and to provide new Guards for their future security.

THINK DEEPER

In what ways does a government guard one's security? Can you think of ways a government might fail to do that?

usurpation: taking something by force

evince: to reveal, to show

despotism: total power (and often in a cruel way)

But if a government attacks the rights of its people and is hungry for total control, the people must replace it.

 THE DEBATE CONTINUES

How a government protects a person's security is still a matter of debate today. Some argue that to care for a person's well-being, the nation needs a larger, more powerful government. Others argue that a smaller, more limited government—one that primarily focuses on protecting freedoms—is more effective. What do you think?

LARGE

SMALL

—Such has been the patient sufferance of these Colonies; and such is now the necessity which **constrains** them to alter their former Systems of Government.

THINK DEEPER

Pretend for a moment that you're King George. Things have certainly been difficult with the colonies in recent years. What a headache! And now you've received this declaration. What might you be thinking? How could this impact your decisions?

constrain: to force; to compel to do something

Egads!*

*Not a direct quote, but hey, you never know.

We've had enough; it's time to swap you with something different.

 INSPIRATION FOR A NEW GOVERNMENT

Once the American Revolution was over, creating something different would be a daunting task. The founders of that government (see page 18) would use their experiences with King George and the philosophies of famous thinkers from the time to shape what that government would look like. Here are a few of those thinkers. You might hear their influence on the Declaration, too!

JOHN LOCKE

Championed a representative government and believed that certain rights were inalienable (see page 14).

CHARLES MONTESQUIEU

Taught that government worked best if power was split up among different branches.

JEAN-JACQUES ROUSSEAU

Insisted that all power ultimately resides with the people, not the ruler (see page 16).

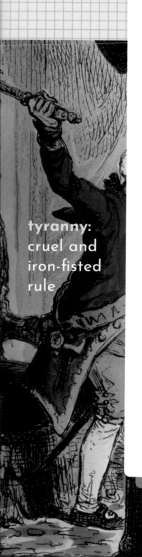

The history of the present King of Great Britain is a history of repeated injuries and usurpations, all having in direct object the establishment of an absolute **Tyranny** over these States. To prove this, let Facts be submitted to a candid world.

tyranny: cruel and iron-fisted rule

 STRONG WORDS

Consider some of the words used in this section: injuries, usurpations, tyranny. Why do you think the writers used such forceful language?

King George has injured us and shown that he wants total power. Don't believe us? Here comes a list.

MEET KING GEORGE III

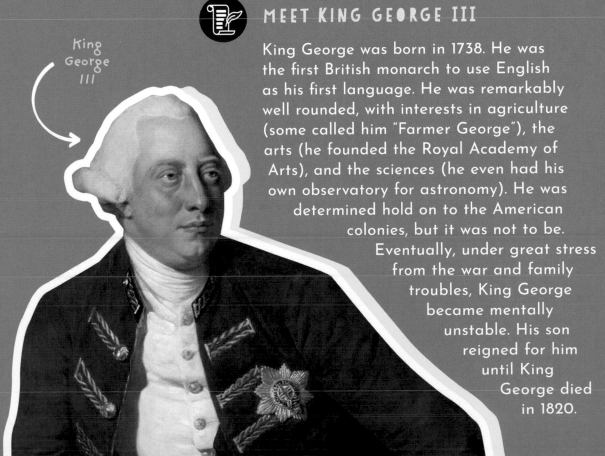

King George III

King George was born in 1738. He was the first British monarch to use English as his first language. He was remarkably well rounded, with interests in agriculture (some called him "Farmer George"), the arts (he founded the Royal Academy of Arts), and the sciences (he even had his own observatory for astronomy). He was determined hold on to the American colonies, but it was not to be. Eventually, under great stress from the war and family troubles, King George became mentally unstable. His son reigned for him until King George died in 1820.

He has refused his **Assent** to Laws, the most wholesome and necessary for the public good.

He has forbidden his Governors to pass Laws of immediate and pressing importance, unless suspended in their operation till his Assent should be obtained; and when so suspended, he has utterly neglected to attend to them.

assent: approval, permission

He hasn't let us pass our own laws—some of which are urgent and important—without his permission. And when we ask for permission, he ignores us.

 ### IGNORING THE COLONIES

After the French and Indian War (see page 3), Great Britain started exerting greater control over the colonies. For example, in 1764, the colony of New York tried to pass a law to include some Native American tribes in the colonies. King George told the colonies to stop pursuing the idea until permission was granted, but then never mentioned it again.

Hey, listen up!

Zzzzz...

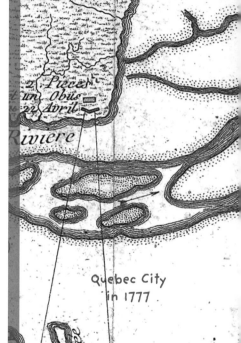

relinquish: to let go of something

inestimable: of great worth

He has refused to pass other Laws for the accommodation of large districts of people, unless those people would **relinquish** the right of Representation in the Legislature, a right **inestimable** to them and formidable to tyrants only.

Quebec City in 1777

He won't let some regions pass laws unless they give up a representative government.

THE QUEBEC QUESTION

In Quebec, a colony under British rule in Canada, King George replaced the representative government with a smaller council directly under his control. This gave him greater power, and some colonists feared he might do something similar in the American colonies. Quebec would be yet another sticking point later on (see page 62).

Quebec

Eh?

Thirteen colonies

He has called together legislative bodies at places unusual, uncomfortable, and distant from the depository of their public Records, for the sole purpose of fatiguing them into compliance with his measures.

The Boston Tea Party (see page 4)

Tea

He moved the location of our governments far away from the people so it would be exhausting just to get there.

The colony's seat of government was moved 25 miles (about a full day's trip) away to Salem.

PUNISHING BOSTON

After the Boston Tea Party, Great Britain moved Massachusetts's government from Boston to Salem. This was incredibly frustrating to the colonists, who saw it as a punishment designed to make it difficult to get to the government offices. It was also a head scratcher, because all public records were still back in Boston!

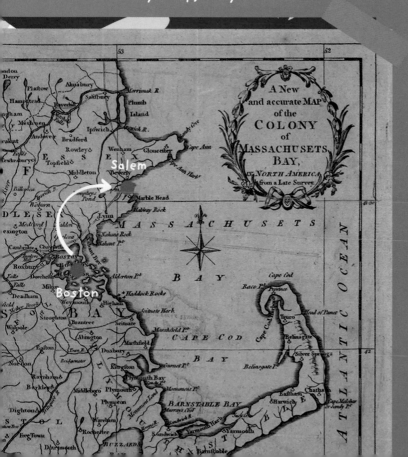

33

He has dissolved Representative Houses repeatedly, for opposing with manly firmness his invasions on the rights of the people.

Patrick Henry speaks in the House of Burgesses, Virginia's assembly (before it was dissolved).

The royal governor, who would have issued the command to disband.

He broke up our local governments, just because they resisted his attacks on the people.

GOODBYE, GOVERNMENT

At various times, and usually to punish the colonies for opposing his rule, King George ordered his royal governors to dissolve their colonial legislatures. This first happened to New York in 1767, then to Massachusetts, then to Virginia (pictured opposite) and North Carolina, and eventually to nearly every colony by the time of the First Continental Congress in 1774.

Cheerio.

King George sends instructions to a royal governor.

The royal governor dissolves the assembly.

The assembly can no longer legally meet.

He has refused for a long time, after such dissolutions, to cause others to be elected; whereby the Legislative powers, incapable of **Annihilation**, have returned to the People at large for their exercise; the State remaining in the mean time exposed to all the dangers of invasion from without, and **convulsions** within.

ELECTIONS CANCELED

BEAT IT

THIS MEANS YOU

annihilation: complete destruction

convulsion: violent chaos

After dissolving our governments, he wouldn't allow new ones to be elected.

WE'LL MEET ANYWAY

Despite having their assemblies dissolved, many colonies—in defiance of royal orders—formed local congresses of their own. These groups raised militias, helped fund the war effort, and sent delegates to the Continental Congress. The British government wasn't pleased. After all, these punishments were meant to create order and bring the colonies back in line.

"Once vigorous measures appear to be the only means left of bringing the Americans to a due submission to the mother country, the colonies will submit."
—King George III

He has endeavoured to prevent the population of these States; for that purpose obstructing the Laws for **Naturalization** of Foreigners; refusing to pass others to encourage their migrations hither, and raising the conditions of new **Appropriations** of Lands.

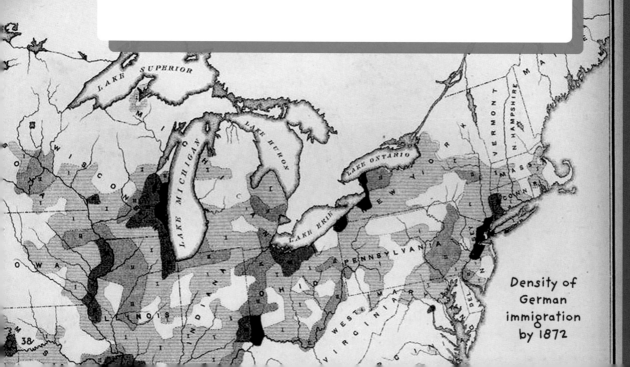

Density of German immigration by 1872

38

He has not allowed immigrants to come to our country and own land.

GERMAN INFLUX

King George was told that large numbers of German immigrants were moving to America. This was true; by 1775, as many as 100,000 Germans had settled in America. This influx concerned the king because he thought those settlers might be sympathetic to the revolution. By stopping them from owning more land in America, he hoped to prevent more support for the revolution. (He also hired German mercenaries, but more on that on page 69.)

Germany's influence in America can still be felt today. Christmas trees, Santa Claus, the Easter Bunny, kindergarten, and even physical education at school largely began with German immigrants.

naturalization: the process of becoming a citizen

appropriation: ownership

Bitte sehr im voraus!

He has obstructed the Administration of Justice, by refusing his Assent to Laws for establishing Judiciary powers.

He has made Judges dependent on his Will alone, for the **tenure** of their offices, and the amount and payment of their salaries.

tenure: holding a position

He took over our judicial system.

He made our judges depend on *him* for their paychecks.

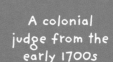

A colonial judge from the early 1700s

JUDGE *THIS*

In Massachusetts, King George took control of the court system (see page 59). One of the ways he did this was by paying the judges himself instead of letting the people pay them. As you might imagine, this put pressure on local judges to cooperate with King George's decrees.

He has erected a **multitude** of New Offices, and sent hither swarms of Officers to harrass our people, and eat out their substance.

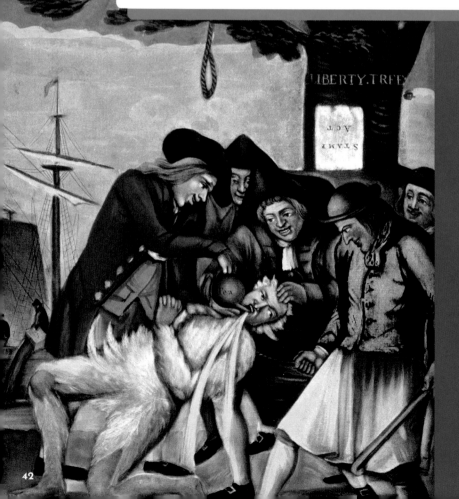

The colonists were not fans of the British tax collectors. This illustration from 1774 depicts the tarring and feathering of a tax collector in Boston. Unfortunately, this kind of thing really happened.

He sent tons of officers to persecute us, and yet we have to feed and support them.

Check, please.

SWARMS OF OFFICERS

By "officers," the colonists are referring to government employees sent to America to do King George's bidding. There were tax collectors, bureaucrats, and council officials who all had to be supported by the colonists. Naturally, this was *not* popular.

multitude: a large number

He has kept among us, in times of peace, Standing Armies without the Consent of our legislatures.

BON VOYAGE!

NO ONE LIKES LOBSTER, ANYWAY

GO HOME

GO HOME, TROOPS

During the French and Indian War (see page 3), Great Britain sent thousands of troops to America to fight. After the war, however, many of the troops were ordered to stay put. This unnerved the colonists. If the war was over, why were the troops still needed? The colonists suspected that King George was trying to gain more control.

There's no war, yet he's kept soldiers here without our permission.

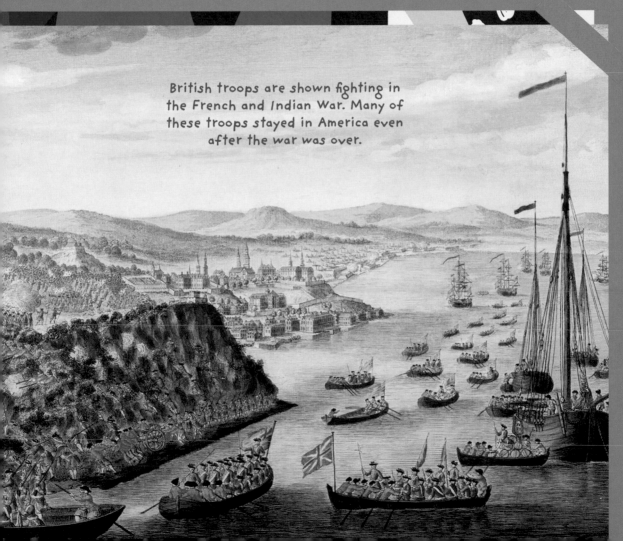

British troops are shown fighting in the French and Indian War. Many of these troops stayed in America even after the war was over.

He has **affected** to render the Military independent of and superior to the Civil power.

MILITARY MIGHT

affected: caused

martial law: when ordinary government is replaced by military control

Having dissolved the Massachusetts assembly (see page 35), King George told the colonists that they had to obey the orders of the military—specifically, General Gage, the British commander in chief. For a people used to governing themselves, this felt an awful lot like **martial law.**

He says we have to obey
the military instead of
our own government.

General
Thomas
Gage

MEET GENERAL GAGE

After the French and Indian War, General Thomas Gage was made commander in chief of British forces in North America. In 1774, he was also appointed royal governor of Massachusetts, thus gaining command of both the British army and the colonial government. Interestingly, Thomas Gage and George Washington served alongside each other in the British army during the French and Indian War (see page 3). Some historians suggest there may have even been some level of friendship between the two men before the revolution. Following a costly win at Bunker Hill, Gage was recalled to England and replaced with General William Howe. Gage and Washington never did engage in battle against each other.

"America is a mere bully, from one end to the other."

He has combined with others to subject us to a jurisdiction foreign to our constitution, and unacknowledged by our laws; giving his Assent to their Acts of pretended Legislation:

Bad luck, old boy.

 ## THE BRITISH PARLIAMENT

The British Parliament first began in the 1200s as a body of local lords who advised the British king (and helped fund his wars). Over time, it developed into a two-house legislature with a House of Lords and a House of Commons. Many of the taxes and policies that infuriated the colonists were the actions of Parliament, not the king. It was for this reason, although much of the Declaration of Independence was directed at King George, that the colonists also singled out Parliament for their anger later on (see page 77).

He has let **Parliament** make laws without our permission. For example . . .

Parliament: the British legislature

The House of Commons, as depicted in 1709

49

For **Quartering** large bodies of armed troops among us:

quarter: to station or shelter

BRITISH "LOBSTERS"

By this time, Great Britain had sent thousands of extra troops to the colonies. These soldiers were extremely unpopular among the colonists, who called them "lobsters" and "bloody backs" because of the red coats they wore. It appears that the name "lobsterback," often used in fictional depictions of the revolution, might not have been invented until the 1800s—several decades after the war. In any case, "lobster" was a fitting insult at the time; lobster was considered low-life peasant food, sometimes even used as fertilizer.

Eating lobster? *That'll* never catch on.

Infamous red jacket

They have sent huge
numbers of soldiers here.

Light infantry	Light infantry	Light infantry
Grenadiers	Grenadiers	Grenadiers
Regiment	Regiment	Regiment

Brigade

A regiment had 10 companies—8
standard, 2 specialized—and
totaled 642 soldiers.

A brigade usually consisted
of 2–4 regiments, also
called battalions.

For protecting them, by a **mock** Trial, from punishment for any Murders which they should commit on the Inhabitants of these States:

mock: pretend, made up

FAIR TRIAL?

In the years preceding the American Revolution, several British soldiers were accused of killing colonists. In two cases—one in Maryland and another in North Carolina—though the soldiers were charged with murder, they were acquitted and let go.

This colonial illustration of the Boston Massacre makes the British look completely at fault.

Engrav'd Printed & Sold by PAUL REVERE BOSTON

Unhappy Boston! see thy Sons deplore,   If scalding drops fromRage from AnguishWrung But know Fate summons to that awful Goal

> They protected those soldiers with a pretend trial, even though some murdered our people.

WHAT ABOUT THE BOSTON MASSACRE?

Though perhaps the most famous incident of British violence against colonial citizens, the Boston Massacre was a confusing affair and probably not implicated in this part of the Declaration. In this event, a rowdy crowd of colonists heckled British troops, going so far as to throw rocks and other objects at the soldiers. Then someone—and no one really knows who—yelled, "Fire!" Five colonists died, and several soldiers were charged with their killings. John Adams (see page 86), though a staunch patriot, defended the soldiers in court in an effort to show the British that the colonists were reasonable and could conduct a fair trial. Two of the soldiers were convicted of manslaughter.

Among those killed was a Black man named Crispus Attucks, who some have called the first casualty of the American Revolution. This is an artist's interpretation of what he might have looked like.

For cutting off our Trade with all parts of the world:

TRADE WARS

The colonies hated all the new British taxes (see page 57), and one way to avoid them was by buying goods from other countries (or **smuggling** goods in and out). Naturally, Parliament didn't want that to happen. They wanted the colonies to be dependent on Great Britain alone, which would mean more leverage over the colonies and more money in taxes.

trade: buying and selling goods

smuggle: to ship goods in secret

Before joining the colonial army (and betraying his country), Benedict Arnold worked for some time as a smuggler.

They didn't let us trade with the rest of the world.

EXPORTS

The colonies produced many goods that they could sell to other parts of the world. These are exports.

Iron

Lumber

Fur

Rice

Rum

Tobacco

IMPORTS

But there were some goods that couldn't be made and had to be bought from other countries. These are imports.

Furniture

Tea

Textiles

Luxuries

Sugar

Manufactured goods

For imposing Taxes on us without our Consent:

Colonists protest the Stamp Act (see page 4), which put a tax on most printed documents and goods.

They made new taxes without our permission.

"No taxation without representation!"

 TAXES, TAXES, TAXES

The colonists were upset that, despite not having a seat in Parliament, they were still *taxed* by Parliament. And what a list of taxes it was! At one time or another, Great Britain taxed the colonists' sugar, molasses, newspapers, almanacs, playing cards, dice, legal documents (like marriage licenses), pamphlets, glass, lead, tea, paper, and paint. There were also laws governing wool and hats and prohibiting colonists from making their own currency.

Lawyer James Otis Jr. was responsible for popularizing the famous phrase about taxes.

For depriving us in many cases, of the benefits of Trial by Jury:

The Magna Carta, often considered the beginning of jury trials in Great Britain

JURY DUTY

Since the 1200s, British law had protected the right to a trial by jury (in some form or another). The jury was to be made up of one's peers from the community. Colonists in America were proud of their right to a jury trial. Indeed, much of the British legal system would be adopted in the formation of America's system.

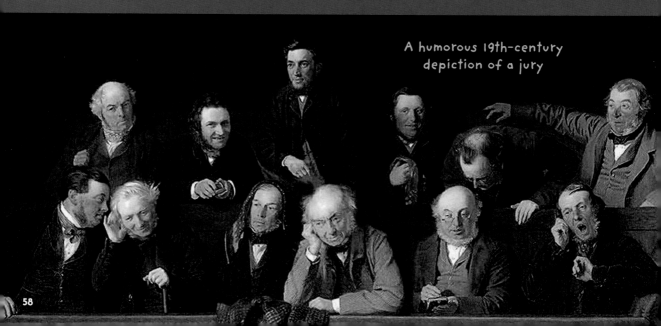

A humorous 19th-century depiction of a jury

They refused to let us have trials by jury.

COURT OF ADMIRALTY

Though the colonists had enjoyed jury trials for some time, Great Britain suddenly set up what were called admiralty courts. In this system, colonists were sent to a single judge (hired by King George, of course) instead of a trial by jury. This was a direct affront to British law and very worrying to the colonists.

THINK DEEPER

What do you think are some of the pros and cons of a trial by jury versus a trial with a single judge?

Women were finally added to all US state juries by 1973.

For transporting us beyond Seas to be tried for pretended offences:

PACK YOUR BAGS

In some cases, Parliament ruled that colonists could be taken to Great Britain for their trial.

off to trial!

They made us stand trial outside our own country and for crimes we didn't commit.

THINK DEEPER

If you were a colonist who had to stand trial, why might you feel uncomfortable about your jury being made of up men from Great Britain instead of the colonies?

This trip could take between six and eight weeks.

For abolishing the free System of English Laws in a neighbouring Province, establishing therein an **Arbitrary** government, and enlarging its Boundaries so as to render it at once an example and fit instrument for introducing the same absolute rule into these Colonies:

LIKE A GOOD NEIGHBOR

Great Britain needed a place to build up its troops as the revolution heated up, and Quebec was the perfect place. It was near the colonies but squarely under British rule (see page 31).

arbitrary: having unrestrained authority

They took complete control of our neighbor, Quebec, all in hopes of doing the same thing here.

Look how large of a border Quebec shared with the Thirteen Colonies at the time of the revolution. Can you see why the colonists were nervous?

CANADA
(THE PROVINCE OF QUEBEC), 1774

━━━ DEFINITE BOUNDARIES
▨▨▨ INDEFINITE BOUNDARIES
▨▨▨ FRENCH FISHING RIGHTS

You just wait until your father comes home.

For taking away our Charters, abolishing our most valuable Laws, and altering fundamentally the Forms of our Governments:

For suspending our own Legislatures, and declaring themselves invested with power to legislate for us in all cases whatsoever.

YOU'RE GROUNDED!

Not only did Parliament dissolve colonial legislatures (see page 35), but in some places, they also got rid of town meetings, stopped the election of jurors, and rewrote parts of colonial constitutions. This was all in an effort to punish the colonists, whom King George felt were like wayward children in need of discipline.

They destroyed our laws and dissolved our governments. Now they say *they're* in charge.

A British political cartoon from 1777 depicts Great Britain as a hobbling old man trying to take charge of his unruly children in America.

He has **abdicated** Government here, by declaring us out of his Protection and waging War against us.

He has plundered our seas, ravaged our Coasts, burnt our towns, and destroyed the lives of our people.

A painting of the British attack on Bunker Hill

Not only has he not protected us, but he has warred *against* us! He's attacked our ships, burned our towns, and ruined our people's lives.

 MASSACHUSETTS MAYHEM

Many of the British attacks mentioned here were on Massachusetts, which Great Britain saw as a hotbed of revolt. By this time, conflicts like the Boston Massacre (see page 53), the Battles of Lexington and Concord, and the Battle of Bunker Hill had already happened. General Gage (see page 47), leader of the British forces, was stationed in Boston. But instead of blaming Massachusetts (it had, after all, been home to the Boston Tea Party), the other colonies rallied around it and came to its defense.

abdicate: to give up responsibility for something

He is at this time transporting large Armies of foreign **Mercenaries** to compleat the works of death, desolation and tyranny, already begun with circumstances of Cruelty & perfidy scarcely paralleled in the most barbarous ages, and totally unworthy the Head of a civilized nation.

mercenary: a soldier who fights for pay (though it should be noted that in this case, these soldiers were essentially rented out by the German princes that governed them and didn't have much say in the matter)

Hired armies are on the way to continue his acts of destruction. This is *hardly* how a king should behave!

HESSIANS

King George hired 30,000 German **mercenaries** to help fight against the colonists. Often called "Hessians," these German soldiers were highly trained and generally feared. Historians estimate that nearly half didn't return home after the war. Some died during the conflict, but others stayed behind to enjoy a new life in America. There were, after all, many German neighbors (see page 39) to call friends!

Hessian troops in 1784, just after the war

He has constrained our fellow Citizens taken Captive on the high Seas to bear Arms against their Country, to become the executioners of their friends and Brethren, or to fall themselves by their Hands.

The "lucky" man being forced to join the British navy

Notice the ship?

He has forced our citizens captured at sea to fight against their own people or be killed.

FORCED TO FIGHT FOR THE ENEMY

The British navy routinely captured American ships and forced the crewmembers to serve on its own ships instead. This is called **impressment**. It was an issue during the revolution, but it became even more troublesome afterward and was a major factor in the buildup to the War of 1812. (The British needed sailors so badly that they also pressed their own citizens into service, as shown in the 1780 illustration opposite.)

impressment:
forcing a person into military service

All this isn't to say the Americans were totally helpless. John Paul Jones, a revolutionary sea captain, gave the British plenty of trouble on the waves!

He has excited **domestic** insurrections amongst us, and has endeavoured to bring on the inhabitants of our frontiers, the merciless Indian Savages, whose known rule of warfare, is an undistinguished destruction of all ages, sexes and conditions.

HARSH WORDS, HARSHER TREATMENT

domestic: at home

Referring to Native Americans as "Indian Savages" was undeniably harsh. It's true that the colonists had just come off a brutal fight with them in the French and Indian War (see page 3), but unfortunately, this was still a common opinion even years later. For much of the next century, in one of the saddest chapters of American history, Native Americans would be driven from their homelands and resettled in other parts of the country.

If you were part of the US government today, would you try to make amends? What might you do?

He's also stirring up fights against us from some of our own citizens and neighboring Native Americans.

NATIVE AMERICANS DURING THE WAR

Native Americans generally tried to stay out of the war. But in some cases, they did take sides and help in the fight. The British often had more success in recruiting Native Americans to their side. This is largely because after the French and Indian War, the British had tried to set boundaries around how far west the colonists could settle, protecting Native Americans' lands. The colonists, on the other hand, aggressively sought to claim those lands.

Thayendanegea led his people against the colonists.

petition: to ask for help

redress: compensation, making things right

In every stage of these Oppressions We have **Petitioned** for **Redress** in the most humble terms: Our repeated Petitions have been answered only by repeated injury. A Prince whose character is thus marked by every act which may define a Tyrant, is unfit to be the ruler of a free people.

THINK DEEPER

There were many voices during the revolution. Some, like John Adams (see page 86), were fiery and direct. Others, like John Jay (see opposite page), were thoughtful and deliberative. How did each play a role? What could have happened if one of those voices were missing?

We have asked him many, *many* times to make these things right. Instead, he attacks us even more. He is truly a tyrant!

THE ROLE OF MODERATES

moderate: someone who doesn't agree with extremes on either side

Moderate voices played an important part in the American Revolution. Despite some early calls for independence, the colonists, urged by people like John Jay, did seek reconciliation with King George first. As Britain ignored these attempts and war looked increasingly likely, Jay and others eventually concluded that independence was the only way forward. Their thoughtful, measured approach helped sway others to the side of revolution.

John Jay later became the first chief justice of the Supreme Court.

Nor have We been wanting in attentions to our Brittish brethren. We have warned them from time to time of attempts by their legislature to extend an unwarrantable jurisdiction over us. We have reminded them of the circumstances of our emigration and settlement here. We have appealed to their native justice and magnanimity, and we have conjured them by the ties of our common kindred to disavow these usurpations, which, would inevitably interrupt our connections and correspondence. They too have been deaf to the voice of justice and of **consanguinity**. We must, therefore, acquiesce in the necessity, which denounces our Separation, and hold them, as we hold the rest of mankind, Enemies in War, in Peace Friends.

The Houses of Parliament

We've also tried asking Parliament to help. We've reminded them that we are brothers, but they've ignored our pleas. They must now be called our enemy.

LORD NORTH

Parliament was deaf to the colonists' pleas. Lord North, the prime minister at the time, felt that giving in to the colonists' demands would only lead to more **concessions** over time. He instead chose to enforce strict obedience to Great Britain, but his strategy ultimately fueled the revolutionary spirit among the colonists.

consanguinity: kinship; sharing a common ancestor

concession: something given up in response to demands

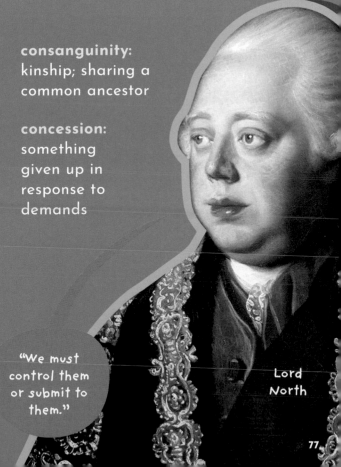

"We must control them or submit to them."

Lord North

We, therefore, the Representatives of the united States of America, in General Congress, Assembled, appealing to the Supreme Judge of the world for the **rectitude** of our intentions, do, in the Name, and by Authority of the good People of these Colonies, **solemnly** publish and declare, That these United Colonies are, and of Right ought to be Free and Independent States;

rectitude: righteousness

solemnly: with dignity and sincerity

We, the representatives of this people, declare that these colonies should be free states.

THINK DEEPER

Now that you've seen the grievances outlined by the colonists, what do you think? Do you agree that they have a right to be "free and independent"? If yes, what do you feel are the most compelling reasons? If no, why do you think so?

This depicts colonists pulling down a statue of King George in New York.

This man is holding a copy of the Declaration (though chances are, most of the people shown in this painting weren't actually there).

that they are **Absolved** from all Allegiance to the British Crown, and that all political connection between them and the State of Great Britain, is and ought to be totally dissolved;

An illustration on the back of the two-dollar bill commemorates the Declaration of Independence being presented to Congress.

We are no longer under the control of King George or Great Britain.

REACTION IN GREAT BRITAIN

As you might expect, this statement didn't go over well on the other side of the Atlantic. Though there were a few who voiced support for the revolution, newspapers from the time generally showed disdain toward the Declaration.

absolved: freed from responsibility

*Yes, this was actually published in The Scots Magazine *in 1776.*

"These gentlemen assume to themselves an unalienable right of talking nonsense."*

YE OLDE NEWS

and that as Free and Independent States, they have full Power to **levy** War, conclude Peace, contract Alliances, establish **Commerce**, and to do all other Acts and Things which Independent States may of right do.

We now have freedom to act as independent states; we can fight wars, find allies, buy and sell goods, and so on.

ACTING AS STATES

It turns out that the new American states would do every one of these things in their fight for independence; they'd fight a yearslong war, make a critical alliance with France, trade, and more. Already, the new nation was well under way.

Benjamin Franklin was key to securing an alliance with France.

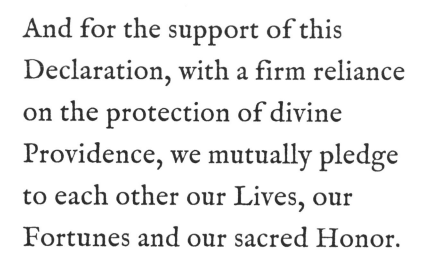

And for the support of this Declaration, with a firm reliance on the protection of divine Providence, we mutually pledge to each other our Lives, our Fortunes and our sacred Honor.

*Historians are unsure if Benjamin Franklin really said this, but it was true nonetheless.

We will support this cause with our lives!

"We must, indeed, all hang together, or assuredly we shall all hang separately."*

WANTED MEN

When the fifty-six signers of the Declaration of Independence said they pledged their lives, they really meant it. In the eyes of Great Britain, they were guilty of treason and worthy of death.

WHAT HAPPENED TO THE SIGNERS?

Each of the fifty-six signers came from different backgrounds and vocations, and their lives after the events of 1776 would be just as varied. Twelve signers would have their homes plundered and destroyed by the British (a sacrifice shared by many of their fellow colonists). Nine would die fighting in the war or from related hardships. Others would live for many years and go on to draft the Constitution or become some of the country's first presidents. Each will always be remembered for playing a vital role in the founding of the United States.

Learn more about what happened to some of the signers below. You can find each on the painting on the previous page by matching up their number and face.

RICHARD STOCKTON was imprisoned by the British and almost starved to death. His home and belongings were destroyed, and he died before the end of the war.

JOHN HANCOCK'S baby girl died when just a few months old, likely from complications resulting from Congress's desperate flight to Baltimore before the advancing British.

JOHN ADAMS would go on to become the second US president. **THOMAS JEFFERSON** would follow as the third president. Though polarized by political differences, both became friends in the end and died on the same day: July 4, 1826, exactly fifty years after the Declaration they had both worked on was adopted by Congress.

RICHARD HENRY LEE, who had officially proposed that Congress declare independence, later served as one of Virginia's first senators to the brand new US Congress under the Constitution.

BENJAMIN FRANKLIN was the only signer to also sign the Constitution and both treaties with Great Britain and France. He is credited with numerous scientific discoveries and inventions.

ROBERT MORRIS used his financial skills (and some of his own money) to help the new nation fund the revolution. He is sometimes called the "Financier of the American Revolution." Sadly, he was extremely poor when he died, having lost his fortune in the 1797 financial crisis.

SAMUEL ADAMS, cousin of John Adams, later became the governor of Massachusetts. He's best known for his role in the Boston Sons of Liberty, where he organized groups like the one involved in the Boston Tea Party (see page 4).

BENJAMIN RUSH was a brilliant doctor who served his country as a field medic during parts of the Revolutionary War and as one of the army's surgeons general.

ROGER SHERMAN, in the words of John Adams, was "one of the most sensible men in the world." Indeed, his common sense would be crucial years later at the Constitutional Convention, during which Sherman proposed a two-house legislature as a compromise between small states and large states. Today, Congress is still set up that way.

THOMAS NELSON JR., according to legend, had his home seized by the British and used as General Charles Cornwallis's headquarters during the Battle of Yorktown. As the story goes, he insisted that Washington still open fire on his own home. Fortunately, that didn't happen, but Nelson did die a few years later from ill health he developed while fighting in the war.

(Not included in painting)

THE DECLARATION'S LEGACY

Bold in its language and lofty in its goals, the Declaration of Independence has lived on for over two hundred years as a guide to freedom and self-government for people all over the world. Today, we're still trying to live up to its most famous charge, that "all men are created equal, that they are endowed by their Creator with certain unalienable Rights, that among these are Life, Liberty and the pursuit of Happiness" (see page 14).

 THINK DEEPER

Imagine you were one of the authors of the Declaration of Independence and were brought to the present day by a time machine.

- What would impress you?
- What would surprise you?
- Would there be things you might wish were different?
- What advice would you give Americans living today?

"We hold these truths to be *self-evident*: that all men and women are created equal . . ."

ELIZABETH CADY STANTON

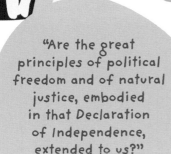

> "Are the great principles of political freedom and of natural justice, embodied in that Declaration of Independence, extended to us?"
>
> FREDERICK DOUGLASS

> "Fourscore and seven years ago our fathers brought forth, on this continent, a new nation, conceived in liberty, and dedicated to the proposition that all men are created equal."
>
> ABRAHAM LINCOLN

AN INSPIRATION FOR CHANGE

Many leaders fighting for equality have found inspiration in the words of the Declaration of Independence. What do **you** feel inspired to do?

> ". . . all men, yes, Black men as well as white men, would be guaranteed the unalienable rights of life, liberty, and the pursuit of happiness."
>
> MARTIN LUTHER KING JR.

SOURCES CONSULTED

"10 Fascinating Facts about the Declaration of Independence." National Constitution Center. https://constitutioncenter.org/blog/10-fascinating-facts-about-the-declaration-of-independence.

"Benjamin Franklin FAQ." The Franklin Institute, October 22, 2019. https://www.fi.edu/benjamin-franklin-faq.

"Benjamin Rush." American Battlefield Trust. https://www.battlefields.org/learn/biographies/benjamin-rush.

"BRIA 20 2 c Hobbes, Locke, Montesquieu, and Rousseau on Government." Constitutional Rights Foundation, 2004. https://www.crf-usa.org/bill-of-rights-in-action/bria-20-2-c-hobbes-locke-montesquieu-and-rousseau-on-government.html.

Brooks, Rebecca Beatrice. "British Soldiers in the Revolutionary War." *History of Massachusetts Blog*, March 7, 2020. https://historyofmassachusetts.org/british-soldiers-revolutionary-war/.

"Building Institutions, Shaping Tastes." Library of Congress. https://www.loc.gov/classroom-materials/immigration/german/building-institutions-shaping-tastes/.

Byron, Matthew A. "Thomas Gage." George Washington's Mount Vernon. https://www.mountvernon.org/library/digitalhistory/digital-encyclopedia/article/thomas-gage/.

"Colonial Travel." Constitution Facts. https://www.constitutionfacts.com/founders-library/colonial-travel/.

Cooper, Kristiina. "A Brief History of the UK Parliament." *BBC News*, September 22, 2014. https://www.bbc.com/news/uk-politics-29252332.

"Decolonization of the Americas." Wikipedia. Wikimedia Foundation, May 7, 2021. https://en.wikipedia.org/wiki/Decolonization_of_the_Americas.

"Documents from the Continental Congress and the Constitutional Convention, 1774-1789." Library of Congress. https://www.loc.gov/collections/continental-congress-and-constitutional-convention-from-1774-to-1789/articles-and-essays/timeline/1764-to-1765/.

Ennis, Daniel James. "Conclusion." 2002. In *Enter the Press-Gang: Naval Impressment in Eighteenth-Century British Literature*, 170. Newark: University of Delaware Press.

Farrell, Stephen. "Politics and Parliament." The History of Parliament. https://www.historyofparliamentonline.org/themes/politics.

"Feudalism." Wikipedia. Wikimedia Foundation, May 12, 2021. https://en.wikipedia.org/wiki/Feudalism.

"French and Indian War/Seven Years' War, 1754-63." U.S. Department of State. U.S. Department of State. https://history.state.gov/milestones/1750-1775/french-indian-war.

"George III (r. 1760-1820)." The Royal Family, August 3, 2018. https://www.royal.uk/george-iii.

The Gettysburg Address. Cornell University. https://rmc.library.cornell.edu/gettysburg/good_cause/transcript.htm.

Gilbert, Dianne. "Destiny of The Signers." https://www.nhccs.org/Destiny.html.

"Hessians." American Battlefield Trust, March 25, 2021. https://www.battlefields.org/learn/articles/hessians.

Hogan, Margaret A., and C. James Taylor. 2011. *The Adams Papers*. Cambridge, Mass: Belknap Press of Harvard Univ. Press.

Horwitz, Tony. "The True Story of the Battle of Bunker Hill." Smithsonian.com. Smithsonian Institution, May 1, 2013. https://www.smithsonianmag.com/history/the-true-story-of-the-battle-of-bunker-hill-36721984/.

Independence Hall Association. "The Declaration of Independence." ushistory.org. Independence Hall Association. https://www.ushistory.org/declaration/lessonplan/index.html.

Italie, Hillel. "Declaration of Independence Still Inspires Activists." *ABC News*, July 1, 2019. https://abcnews.go.com/Entertainment/wireStory/declaration-independence-inspires-activists-64062054.

Jaffee, David, and Megan Mehr. "Native Americans and the American Revolution: Choosing Sides." National Endowment for the Humanities, May 13, 2019. https://edsitement.neh.gov/lesson-plans/native-americans-role-american-revolution-choosing-sides.

"John Jay." American Battlefield Trust. https://www.battlefields.org/learn/biographies/john-jay.

"Join, or Die." Wikipedia. Wikimedia Foundation, May 7, 2021. https://en.wikipedia.org/wiki/Join,_or_Die.

Ketchum, Richard. "England's Vietnam: The American Revolution." *American Heritage*, May 1, 2021. https://www.americanheritage.com/englands-vietnam-american-revolution.

"Lord North." American Battlefield Trust. https://www.battlefields.org/learn/biographies/lord-north.

"Loyalist." *Encyclopædia Britannica*. Britannica Group, Inc. https://www.britannica.com/topic/loyalist.

Makos, Isaac. "Roles of Native Americans during the Revolution." American Battlefield Trust, April 13, 2021. https://www.battlefields.org/learn/articles/roles-native-americans-during-revolution.

"Massachusetts Provincial Congress." Wikipedia. Wikimedia Foundation, February 27, 2021. https://en.wikipedia.org/wiki/Massachusetts_Provincial_Congress.

McGaughy, J. Kent. "Lee, Richard Henry (1732-1794)." *Encyclopedia Virginia*, January 20, 1732. https://encyclopediavirginia.org/entries/lee-richard-henry-1732-1794/.

McKee, Mary. "British Reaction to America's Declaration of Independence." *The British Newspaper Archive Blog*. https://blog.britishnewspaperarchive.co.uk/2017/07/04/british-reaction-to-americas-declaration-of-independence/.

National Geographic Society. "Colonial Trade Routes and Goods." National Geographic Society, March 14, 2014. https://www.nationalgeographic.org/photo/colonial-trade/.

"Nelson House." National Parks Service. U.S. Department of the Interior, August 9, 2015. https://www.nps.gov/york/learn/historyculture/nelson-house.htm.

"On This Day, the Boston Massacre Lights the Fuse of Revolution." National Constitution Center. https://constitutioncenter.org/blog/on-this-day-the-boston-massacre-lights-the-fuse-of-revolution.

"On This Day: 'No Taxation without Representation!'" The National Constitution Center. https://constitutioncenter.org/interactive-constitution/blog/250-years-ago-today-no-taxation-without-representation.

"Robert Morris." American Battlefield Trust. https://www.battlefields.org/learn/biographies/robert-morris.

Robertson, Geoffrey. "Magna Carta and Jury Trial." The British Library. The British Library, February 9, 2015. https://www.bl.uk/magna-carta/articles/magna-carta-and-jury-trial.

"Roger Sherman, Revolutionary and Dedicated Public Servant." Connecticut History, a CTHumanities Project, April 21, 2021. https://connecticuthistory.org/roger-sherman-revolutionary-and-dedicated-public-servant/.

Stanton, Elizabeth Cady. "Seneca Falls Declaration." Digital History. http://www.digitalhistory.uh.edu/disp_textbook.cfm?psid=1087&smtID=3.

"The Connecticut Compromise—Today in History: July 16." Connecticut History, a CTHumanities Project, July 13, 2020. https://connecticuthistory.org/the-connecticut-compromise/.

"The Life of John Jay." John Jay Homestead. http://johnjayhomestead.org/about-john-jay/the-life-of-john-jay/.

"Thomas Gage." American Battlefield Trust. https://www.battlefields.org/learn/biographies/thomas-gage.

"Thomas Jefferson and the Declaration of Independence." Monticello. https://www.monticello.org/thomas-jefferson/jefferson-s-three-greatest-achievements/the-declaration/jefferson-and-the-declaration/.

Uva, Katie. "Benedict Arnold." George Washington's Mount Vernon. https://www.mountvernon.org/library/digitalhistory/digital-encyclopedia/article/benedict-arnold/.

Wilde, Robert. "Germans in the American Revolutionary War." ThoughtCo. https://www.thoughtco.com/germans-american-revolutionary-war-1222023.

Willett-Wei, Megan. "The Remarkable Story of How Lobster Went from Being Used as Fertilizer to a Beloved Delicacy." *Business Insider*. Business Insider, August 16, 2013. https://www.businessinsider.com/the-history-of-gourmet-lobster-2013-8.

ABOUT THE AUTHOR

David Miles is an award-winning author and illustrator of over fifty books, including *The Interactive Constitution, Book, Allegro, Unicorn (and Horse)*, and other titles.

David is also a family descendant of George Walton, one of the signers of the Declaration. When young George's parents died, David's great-great-great-great aunt and uncle took George in and raised him. George would later become a lawyer, attend the Second Continental Congress, sign the Declaration, and serve as governor of Georgia. He was one of the few signers to not own slaves.

David has been named a Cybils Awards finalist, *Publishers Weekly* Star Watch nominee, TRVST Changemaker, New York Book Show award winner, and Bill Fisher Award finalist, among other accolades. He lives in Fresno, California, with his family.

 If you liked this book, please leave a review online at your favorite retailer. Honest reviews spread the word about Bushel & Peck—and help us make better books, too!

ABOUT BUSHEL & PECK BOOKS

Bushel & Peck Books is a children's publishing house with a special mission. Through our Book-for-Book Promise™, we donate one book to kids in need for every book we sell. Our beautiful books are given to kids through schools, libraries, local neighborhoods, shelters, nonprofits, and also to many selfless organizations who are working hard to make a difference. So thank you for purchasing this book! Because of you, another book will make its way into the hands of a child who needs it most.

NOMINATE A SCHOOL OR ORGANIZATION TO RECEIVE FREE BOOKS

Do you know a school, library, or organization that could use some free books for their kids? We'd love to help! Please fill out the nomination form on our website and we'll do everything we can to make something happen.

www.bushelandpeckbooks.com/pages/
nominate-a-school-or-organization

truths to be self-evident, that all men are created equal, that they are endowed by their Creator

—— That to secure these rights, Governments are instituted among Men, deriving their just

one of these ends, it is the Right of the People to alter or to abolish it, and to institute new

to them shall seem most likely to effect their Safety and Happiness. Prudence, indeed,

and accordingly all experience hath shewn, that mankind are more disposed to suffer, while

But when a long train of abuses and usurpations, pursuing invariably the same Object

such Government, and to provide new Guards for their future security. —— Such has

their former Systems of Government. The history of the present King of Great

of an absolute Tyranny over these States. To prove this, let Facts be submitted to a candid

the public good. —— He has forbidden his Governors to pass Laws of immediate

and when so suspended, he has utterly neglected to attend to them. —— He has refused to

the right of Representation in the Legislature, a right inestimable to them and formidable

distant from the depository of their Public Records, for the sole purpose of fatiguing them into

with manly firmness his invasions on the rights of the people. —— He has refused for

of Annihilation, have returned to the People at large for their exercise; the State remain

—— He has endeavoured to prevent the Population of these States; for that purpose obstruc-

and raising the conditions of new Appropriations of Lands. —— He has obstructed the

He has made Judges dependent on his Will alone, for the tenure of their offices, and the amount

swarms of Officers to harrass our people, and eat out their substance. —— He has kept among

the Military independent of and superior to the Civil power. —— He has combined

giving his Assent to their Acts of pretended Legislation: —— For quartering large bodies of

which they should commit on the Inhabitants of these States: —— For cutting off

depriving us in many cases, of the benefits of Trial by Jury; —— For transporting us beyond

neighbouring Province, establishing therein an Arbitrary government, and enlarging its Boundaries

these Colonies: —— For taking away our Charters, abolishing our most valuable Laws, and

declaring themselves invested with power to legislate for us in all cases whatsoever.

—— He has plundered our seas, ravaged our Coasts, burnt our towns, and destroyed the Lives

works of death, desolation and tyranny, already begun with circumstances of Cruelty & perfidy

He has constrained our fellow Citizens taken Captive on the high Seas to bear Arms against

—— He has excited domestic insurrections amongst us, and has endeavoured to bring on the

destruction of all ages, sexes and conditions. In every stage of these Oppressions We

injury. A Prince, whose character is thus marked by every act which may define a Tyrant,

We have warned them from time to time of attempts by their legislature to extend an unwarrant-

We have appealed to their native justice and magnanimity, and we have conjured them

connections and correspondence. They too have been deaf to the voice of justice and of

hold them, as we hold the rest of mankind, Enemies in War, in Peace Friends. ——

Congress, Assembled, appealing to the Supreme Judge of the world for the rectitude of our in-

declare, That these United Colonies are, and of Right ought to be Free and Independent

armed troops among us: — For protecting them, by a mock Trial from punishment for any ... our Trade with all parts of the world: — For imposing Taxes on us without our Consent: — ... Seas to be tried for pretended offences ——— For abolishing the free System of English Laws in a ... so as to render it at once an example and fit instrument for introducing the same absolute rule ... altering fundamentally the Forms of our Governments: — For suspending our own Legislat... He has abdicated Government here, by declaring us out of his Protection and waging War again... of our people. ——— He is at this time transporting large Armies of foreign Mercenaries to compleat ... scarcely paralleled in the most barbarous ages, and totally unworthy the Head of a civilized nation. ... their Country, to become the executioners of their friends and Brethren, or to fall themselves by their ... inhabitants of our frontiers, the merciless Indian Savages, whose known rule of warfare, is an undistin... have Petitioned for Redress in the most humble terms: Our repeated Petitions have been answered by ... is unfit to be the ruler of a free people. Nor have We been wanting in attentions to our British ... able jurisdiction over us. We have reminded them of the circumstances of our emigration and settle... by the ties of our common kindred to disavow these usurpations, which, would inevitably inter... consanguinity. We must, therefore, acquiesce in the necessity, which denounces our Separation... We, therefore, the Representatives of the united States of America, in G... tentions, do, in the Name, and by Authority of the good People of these Colonies, solemnly publish... States; that they are Absolved from all Allegiance to the British Crown, and that all political... that as Free and Independent States, they have full Power to levy War, conclude Peace, cont... States may of right do. ——— And for the support of this Declaration, with a firm relia... and our sacred Honor.

John H...

Button Gwinnett
Lyman Hall
Geo Walton.

Wm Hooper
Joseph Hewes,
John Penn

Edward Rutledge

Th...
Thomas Ly...
Arthur Middleton

Samuel Cha...
Wm Paca
Thos Ston...
Charles Carroll...

George ...
Richard ...
Th Jeff...

Benj Harr...
Th. Nelson ...
Francis Lightf...
Carter Braxt...